The Dodo Is Dead

and other questions about extinct and endangered animals

Andrew Charman

KINGFISHER

KINGFISHER

Published 2013 by Kingfisher
an imprint of Macmillan Children's Books
a division of Macmillan Publishers Limited
20 New Wharf Road, London N1 9RR
Basingstoke and Oxford
Associated companies throughout the world
www.panmacmillan.com

First published 1996 by Kingfisher

Consultants: Andrew Branson, Michael Chinery,
David Burnie

ISBN 978-0-7534-3274-7

Copyright © Macmillan Children's Books 2013

9 8 7 6 5 4 3 2 1

1TR/0912/UTD/WKT/140MA

A CIP catalogue record for this book is available from
the British Library.

Printed in China.

Illustrations: John Butler 18–19; Mike Davis 13bl; Peter Dennis
(Linda Rogers Associates) 24–25; Christian Hook 30–31; Biz
Hull (Artist Partners) 28–29; Ian Jackson 12–13, 16–17, 20–21;
Tony Kenyon (BL Kearley) all cartoons (except 13bl); Terence
Lambert 22–23; Alan Male (Linden Artists) 14–15; Nicki Palin
6–7; Maurice Pledger (Bernard Thornton Artists) 10–11; Bryan
Poole 4–5; David Wright (Kathy Jakeman) cover, 8–9, 26–27.

CONTENTS

Why are there no dinosaurs on Earth?

Animals can become extinct because of things that people do or because the places they live in change.

The dinosaurs lived on Earth for millions of years. Then, about 65 million years ago, they became extinct – every single one of them disappeared. No one knows exactly why, but one idea is that a giant asteroid crashed into Earth. As a result the climate changed and the world became too cold for the dinosaurs.

Do all animals die out?

Every kind of animal dies out eventually. But new kinds of animal usually appear to take their place. These new species are often descendants of the extinct ones. For example, the elephants on Earth today are related to the hairy mammoths that disappeared about 10,000 years ago.

Many animals are endangered, that is, in danger of dying out, because people have hunted too many of them, or are still hunting them.

When harmful chemicals get into the air, soil or water they can cause pollution. This can poison so many animals that the species becomes endangered.

When people move to new parts of the world they often take animals with them. These new animals sometimes hunt the ones that already live there.

Some animals are endangered because the places in which they live are cleared to make room for farms, factories, roads or houses.

5

Why is the dodo dead?

Dodos lived on the island of Mauritius in the Indian Ocean until they all died out in about 1680. Many were killed by hungry sailors who visited the island. The poor birds weren't used to hunters and were slow to escape because they couldn't fly.

The elephant bird was the largest bird that has ever lived. Its eggs were 200 times bigger than a chicken's egg! It died out about 300 years ago.

The dodo laid its eggs on the ground, which made them easy pickings for hungry dogs or rats!

Which extinct animal looked half-horse, half-zebra?

Magnificent herds of quaggas once roamed across the grassy plains of southern Africa. But they were shot by settlers for their unusual skins and for meat. So many were killed that, by 1883, there was not a single quagga left.

In England in the early 19th century, it was fashionable to have quaggas pulling your carriage.

The last Tasmanian wolf, or thylacine, died in 1936. It was a strange mixture of a beast. It looked as if it had the head of a wolf, the stripes of a tiger and the tail of a kangaroo!

How many creepy-crawlies are there?

So far, we have found around one million different kinds of creepy-crawly – more than any other type of creature. Yet many insects are at risk of extinction. If we go on destroying the places where these animals live, many will disappear forever – some before they've even been discovered.

The rare Queen Alexandra's birdwing butterfly lives in Papua New Guinea. But its forest home is being cleared.

There are so many creepy-crawlies, it is impossible to look after each one. The best way to save insects is to protect the places where they live.

The Lord Howe Island stick insect was once one of the most rare insects in the world. It was thought to be extinct but in 2003, scientists found about 30 of them on a tiny island called Ball's Pyramid, near Australia. By 2012, the captive population had grown to many thousands.

Which endangered insect is bigger than a mouse?

The giant weta is a large, wingless insect – three times bigger than a mouse! It's become endangered because so much of its forest home in New Zealand has been cleared and because it is hunted by rats. Now the giant weta is protected in nature reserves.

Red-kneed tarantulas may look scary, but they're harmless to us. They are endangered because so many are taken from the wild to become pets.

Why do animals like wetlands?

A boggy marsh or swamp provides a home and plenty of food for all sorts of different creatures. But wetlands are not being preserved. Many areas are drained to make way for farms or housing. All wetland animals will be under threat if their homes continue to disappear.

Wetlands are good food-stops for birds that fly long distances. They often stop over on long flights to rest or feed before going on with their journey.

Whooping crane

Snail kite

Beaver

Key deer

Leon Springs pupfish

Aquatic box turtle

American alligators were once hunted for their skins. By the 1960s they were endangered and the hunting was stopped. Now their numbers are rising again.

Which orphans are fed by puppets?

In some Russian wetlands, people are caring for Siberian crane chicks who have no parents. These human 'mums' wear sheets over their heads and puppets on their hands. The chicks think they're being looked after by real birds and are more likely to join a real flock when they grow up.

Wood stork

Schaus's swallowtail butterfly

Green heron

Marbled teal

Apache trout

American crocodile

11

Why are boats bad for manatees?

Manatees are gentle animals – they spend their life cruising along, grazing on sea grass. Unfortunately, it's not only the manatees that enjoy a cruise. They share their waterways with fast-moving boats. Many manatees are cut by propeller blades and the animals are getting rarer.

Some scientists believe that just a few Chinese river dolphins still exist, but they may already be extinct. These creatures are almost blind, and use sound to find food. The sound of boat engines can confuse them, and cause them to swim the wrong way – sometimes into fishing nets.

Where do sturgeon eggs go?

Every year sturgeons swim from the sea to the rivers where they were born, to lay their eggs. Many don't make it – they are caught for their eggs. The eggs are sold as a luxury food called caviar.

Why should you keep quiet about olms?

Animal collectors have taken so many olms from underground rivers and pools that they are now very rare. So when people find them in new, safe places, they should keep it a secret.

In a sea-life hospital in the USA, injured manatees are given life-jackets to wear. These help them to stay afloat while they get better.

How can fish make an eagle sick?

In Europe, river otters nearly died out because their rivers were so polluted. But some of the rivers have been cleaned and the otters are coming back at last.

The bald eagle was once close to extinction, after its fish suppers had been poisoned by crop spray. The spray had washed off the land into lakes and inside the fish. Luckily the poison was banned and the birds are thriving again.

13

Which endangered animal has a magic horn?

Rhinos live on the grasslands of Africa and Asia. It is against the law to hunt them, but some people still do. This is because they can get a lot of money for a rhino's horn. In some countries the horn is thought to be magical. It is carved into dagger handles or ground up for medicines.

In some African nature reserves the rangers catch the rhinos and cut off their horns. It doesn't hurt the rhinos, and hopefully it will stop the poachers from killing them.

The African pancake tortoise is endangered because so many are caught and sold as pets. In the wild it gets away from its enemies by hiding between rocks. It may fool other animals, but this trick doesn't work against the hunters.

Where can you shoot elephants?

Elephants are endangered because so many are killed for their ivory tusks. In most places it is against the law to shoot them – except with a camera. The money the tourists pay to see the elephants can be spent on protecting these animals from the poachers.

Like many grassland animals, the great bustard is becoming endangered, as its home is turned into farmland. Cattle trample on the nests, and escaping birds often fly into overhead cables.

Which 'extinct' animal returned to the wild?

Père David's deer were once extinct in the wild. The only ones left lived in zoos and parks. Luckily they were bred so successfully that now they are being returned to their grassland homes in north China.

Why do orang-utans need so many trees?

Orang-utans are rainforest animals that spend all their lives in the trees. When trees are cut down, gaps are left in the forest, and the orang-utans can't move about looking for food or places to sleep.

There are more kinds of tree and animal in the rainforests than in any other place. When the trees are cut down, all the living things in the forests are in danger.

Which endangered animal is the shyest?

The shy okapi is so hard to find that scientists didn't know it existed until 1901! It's difficult to know exactly how many there are but it's estimated that there are only 10,000 to 20,000 left in the wild.

Why is it bad luck to be an aye-aye?

Aye-ayes feed at night in the rainforests of Madagascar. Some of the people of that island think that aye-ayes bring bad luck, so they kill them. The animals are extremely rare, but in some places they are now protected.

Rainforest hunters have used poison from arrow-poison frogs on the tips of their arrows for centuries. But now the frogs may become endangered because so many are being collected to sell as pets.

Which fox flies to its food?

The Rodrigues flying fox isn't a fox at all. It's a bat that lives on Rodrigues Island in the Indian Ocean. It eats fruit, so it needs lots of fruit trees. Most of its forest home has been cut down and there are now only a few thousand of these bats left in the wild.

Why are polar bears still at risk?

Polar bears used to be hunted for their fur. That's stopped now and the biggest threat to them is the planet overheating due to pollution in the air. If the Arctic ice melts, the bears won't be able to roam freely in search of food.

Why do seals get their fur dyed?

In some areas of the Canadian Arctic, the pups of harp seals are hunted for their pure white fur. People trying to protect the seals sometimes spray them with coloured dye. It doesn't hurt the baby seals, but it makes their fur useless to the hunters.

In some areas, polar bears go into towns to scavenge for food. Hungry bears can be a danger to people. Some have to be shot, but most are just taken somewhere safer.

People nearly hunted the musk ox to extinction until they realized they would make more money from its thick, soft fur than its meat. They stopped killing the ox and now comb it for its fur instead.

Which threatened whale has a unicorn's horn?

The narwhal is a kind of whale which lives in the Arctic seas. The male is hunted for his spiralled tusk which looks just like a unicorn's horn. If too many narwhals are taken, they may one day become extinct.

The only people who live in Antarctica are scientists working in research stations. There are no cities or towns. It is the last wilderness and many think it should stay that way.

KEEP OUT OF THE ANTARCTIC

GO AWAY

What's so 'right' about the right whale?

The right whale got its name from the people who used to hunt it, the whalers. They said it was the right whale to catch, because it gave lots of useful whale bone and oil. So many were killed that it became endangered. Most hunting stopped in 1949, but the whales are still very rare.

The Inuit people of the Arctic still hunt right whales. They are allowed to because it is part of their traditional way of life. Some people think this should be stopped too.

Modern fishing boats can catch too many fish. If they carry on taking so many, there'll come a day when all the boats will trawl for the same few fish.

People have always been scared of great white sharks, but the sharks have more reason to be scared of us. Many are hunted every year, and their teeth and jaws are sold to make expensive trinkets.

At certain times large bands of crown-of-thorns sea stars get together to feast on coral. This may be because fishing boats are catching too many of the sea star's natural enemies.

Are there parks in the sea?

We think of parks being on land, but there are lots in the sea. Many underwater parks and reserves have been made to protect the delicate coral reefs. The largest is the Great Barrier Reef, off the coast of Australia. No one is allowed to harm the wildlife there.

Every year millions of sea creatures die because they are trapped in rubbish made of plastic. Turtles often choke on plastic bags, thinking they are yummy jellyfish.

When do parrots make bad pets?

Parrots make bad pets when they are born in the wild. Every year thousands of parrots are taken from their natural home to other countries in tiny, cramped boxes. Many die before they even get there; many more die soon after.

An animal that is taken from its natural home is less likely to survive than one that is born and bred by people. If you want a pet, make sure that it isn't a wild animal.

Spix's macaws have been highly prized as pets. Today there are only around 85 left, but sadly none of them live in the wild. The last known wild Spix's macaw disappeared from north-east Brazil in 2000.

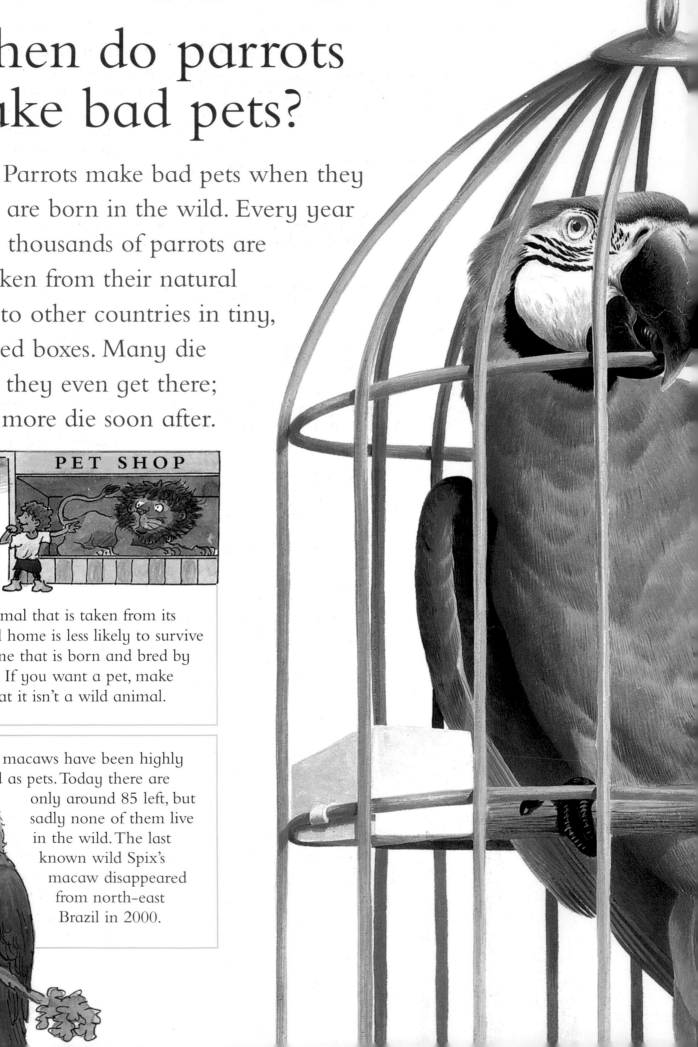

It is a good idea to find out how large your pet will become before you buy it. People are often surprised when the small pet they took home grows into a monster!

Who carries a chameleon in a suitcase?

Holiday-makers have been caught with chameleons in their suitcases. It's against the law to take endangered animals from one country to another. These people wanted to smuggle the lizards home.

Chimps, macaques and tamarins are often kept by scientists who test their new medicines on them. Some people say this has to be done to make sure that medicines are safe for humans. Others say it is cruel and should be stopped.

How could a bonfire save elephants?

The President of Kenya once set fire to 12 tonnes of elephant tusks, worth over £1,500,000. The tusks had been taken away from poachers. By burning them, Kenya was saying to the world that it thought buying and selling ivory was wrong. It was hoping to persuade other countries to stop the trade in ivory and do more to protect elephants.

Who grabs robber crabs?

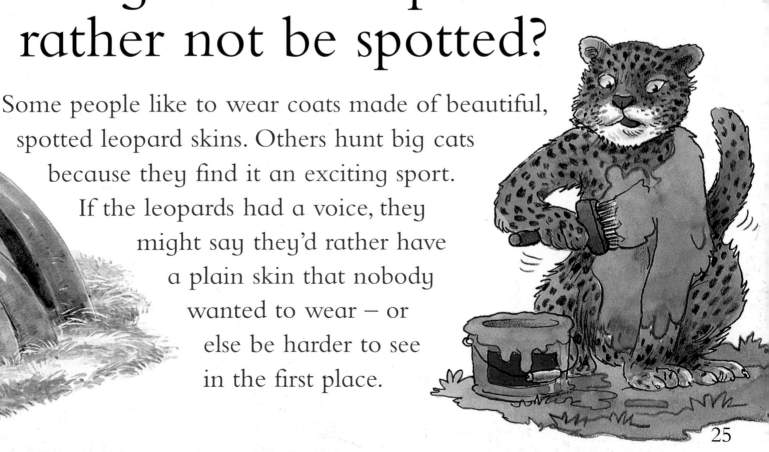

Robber crabs live on islands in the Pacific and Indian Oceans. They grow to one metre in length. They are hunted for food and made into souvenirs for tourists.

At 1.8 metres long, the Chinese giant salamander is the largest salamander in the world. So many people enjoy eating it that it has become endangered.

Why would leopards rather not be spotted?

Some people like to wear coats made of beautiful, spotted leopard skins. Others hunt big cats because they find it an exciting sport. If the leopards had a voice, they might say they'd rather have a plain skin that nobody wanted to wear – or else be harder to see in the first place.

Why do tigers need corridors?

In India, many tigers live in reserves and national parks, where they are safe from hunters. The problem is that one park is often cut off from another. A 'corridor' is a strip of forest linking two parks. Tigers can travel along it to find food or mates.

How does a possum cross the road?

The rare mountain pygmy possum of Australia uses a subway. After a road was built through its reserve, the males kept getting run over when they went to visit the females. Subways were built and now they can cross the roads safely.

The Galápagos Islands in the Pacific Ocean are home to plants and animals not found anywhere else in the world. The islands have been turned into a huge national park, so all the wildlife there is protected.

Why are gorillas not to be sniffed at?

Mountain gorillas live in reserves high up in the Virunga Mountains in Africa. People can visit them, but the gorillas are not used to common human illnesses. They can die of flu. To protect the gorillas, visitors have to keep a safe distance.

There are probably fewer than 2,000 tigers left in India. They are protected by law, but poachers still kill them because their claws and bones can be sold to make medicines, and their fur sells for lots of money too.

When do animals like going to the zoo?

In the past, zoos kept animals just for people to look at. To some people, the animals looked cramped and lonely. Today, many zoos are working hard to breed endangered animals, such as tamarins, and hopefully return them to the wild. If animals could talk, they might say they preferred this kind of zoo.

When do animals like leaving the zoo?

The last wild Arabian oryx was shot in 1972. Luckily, a few were rescued before this and were kept in zoos. They bred well and now a herd of about 1,000 or more roams the deserts of Oman.

Eighty years ago, the golden hamster was nearly extinct. Then one female and her 12 young were caught and allowed to breed in safety. Soon there were millions of them!

Which endangered animal is brought up in a bucket?

Kemp's ridley turtle babies are being raised in special hatcheries in the USA and Mexico. In their buckets, they are safe from seabirds and other hunters. When they are big enough to fend for themselves they are put into the ocean.

Everyone thought the bridled nailtail wallaby, or flashjack, was extinct. Then a colony was discovered in 1973 near Dingo in eastern Australia. The area where they live is now protected.

Why do animals need us?

In most cases, animals become endangered because of things that people do. Animals cannot speak so they need some of us to speak up for them. And then they need us to stop doing the bad things we do, and save them.

Lots of people are helping animals in danger. If there's an oil spill, for example, teams work hard to clean the animals so that they can be returned to the wild.

SAVE THE WHALE

NO FUR

SAVE THE RAINFOREST

RECYCLE NOW

Everyone can help to save endangered animals. We can join groups that are trying to protect them. We can be careful about the things we buy, and we can take less from the natural world, pollute less and recycle more.

Why do we need animals?

Some wild animals provide us with food, clothing and other materials. If they disappear, we'll lose those things. Some animals may be useful to us in ways we don't yet know. Also, animals make the world a beautiful and interesting place. If we lose them, it shows how little we care – for them, for the world and for ourselves.

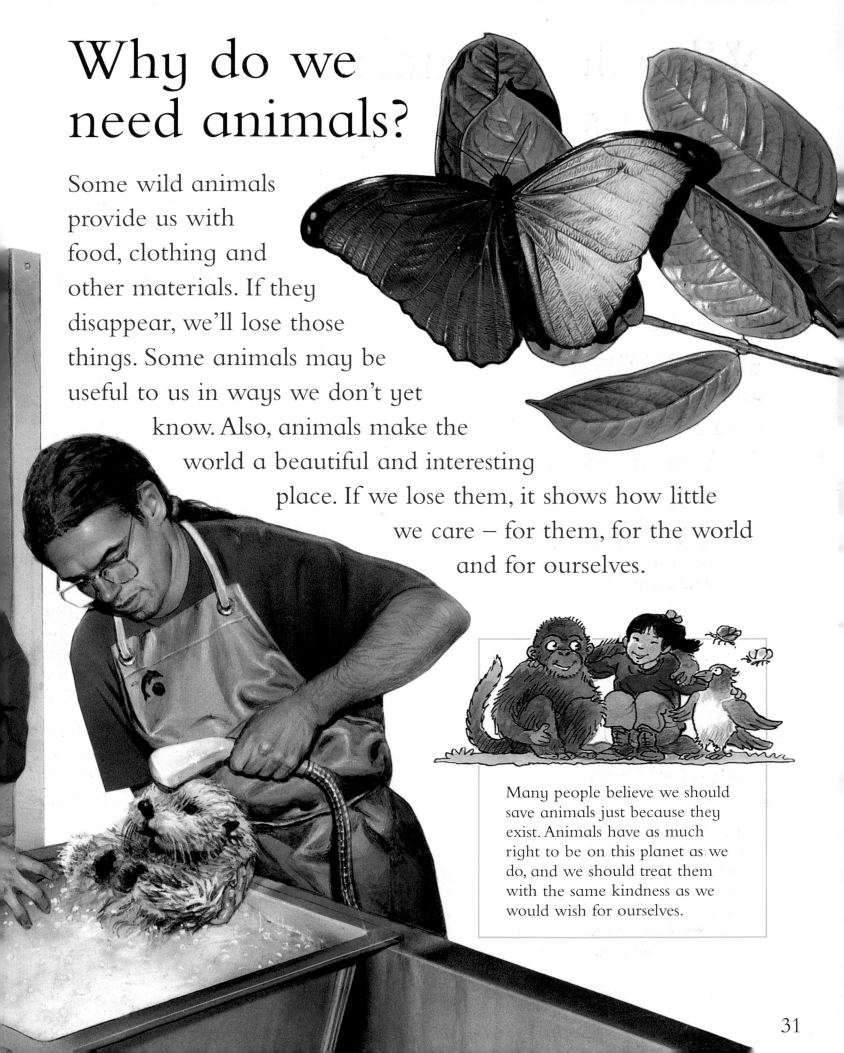

Many people believe we should save animals just because they exist. Animals have as much right to be on this planet as we do, and we should treat them with the same kindness as we would wish for ourselves.

Index